Cool

BIRDS & BUGS

Great Things to Do in the Great Outdoors

Katherine Hengel

Checkerboard Library

An Imprint of Abdo Publishing
abdopublishing.com

abdopublishing.com

Published by Abdo Publishing, a division of ABDO,
PO Box 398166, Minneapolis, Minnesota 55439.
Copyright © 2016 by Abdo Consulting Group, Inc.
International copyrights reserved in all countries. No
part of this book may be reproduced in any form without
written permission from the publisher. Checkerboard
Library™ is a trademark and logo of Abdo Publishing.

Printed in the United States of America,
North Mankato, Minnesota
062015
092015

Content Developer: Nancy Tuminelly
Design and Production: Jen Schoeller, Mighty Media, Inc.
Series Editor: Liz Salzmann
Photo Credits: Frankie and Maclean Potts, Jen Schoeller,
Shutterstock

The following manufacturers/names appearing in
this book are trademarks: Craft Smart®, L'eggs® Sheer
Energy®, Market Pantry™, Scribbles®, Sharpie®

Library of Congress Cataloging-in-Publication Data
Hengel, Katherine, author.
  Cool birds & bugs : great things to do in the great
outdoors / Katherine Hengel.
     pages cm. -- (Cool great outdoors)
  Audience: Grades 3 to 6.
  Includes index.
  ISBN 978-1-62403-694-1
1. Bird watching--Juvenile literature.
2. Bird attracting--Juvenile literature.
3. Butterfly watching--Juvenile literature. 4. Butterfly
attracting--Juvenile literature. I. Title. II. Title: Birds &
bugs. III. Title: Cool birds and bugs.
  QL676.2.H456 2016
  598.07234--dc23
                          2014045309

To Adult Helpers:

This is your chance to inspire kids to
get outside! As children complete the
activities in this book, they'll develop new
skills and confidence. They'll even learn
to love and appreciate the great outdoors!

Some of the activities in this book will
require your help, but encourage kids to
do as much as they can on their own. Be
there to offer guidance when needed, but
mostly be a cheerleader for their creative
spirit and natural inspirations!

Before getting started, it helps to review
the activities and set some ground
rules. Remind kids that cleaning up is
mandatory! Adult supervision is always
recommended. So is going outside!

Key Symbols:

In this book you may see these symbols.
Here is what they mean:

HOT STUFF!
This project requires the use of a
stove, oven, or campfire. Always use
pot holders when handling hot objects.

SHARP!
This project requires the use of a
sharp object. Get help.

CONTENTS

Wild Life!

There are a lot of small creatures living outdoors. You may not have even noticed them. But they can be fascinating to watch. Start looking for interesting birds and bugs when you are outside.

We spend most of our lives inside. Take a second to count the hours. You sleep inside. You eat inside. You study inside. That's life in the 21st century.

You've got to get out!

There are many ways to enjoy birds and bugs. You can make homemade bird feeders. You can make your own bug jar! It all happens outside. And it's all good. They don't call it the great **outdoors** for nothing!

A NATURAL RECHARGE!

What's so great about the great outdoors? A lot! Being outside exposes us to the sun's natural light. The sun gives us **vitamin** D. Vitamin D keeps our bodies strong! Exposure to sunlight helps regulate our sleeping patterns. The more you are outside, the easier it is to fall asleep!

Here Birdie, Birdie!

*N*ature can seem far away. Birds and bugs don't exactly come when called. It's hard to get a good look at them. But there are things you can do to attract them.

You can set out food and other materials that animals need. It might cause them to come closer. The closer they are, the more you can understand and appreciate them!

Meeting Animals on Their Own Turf

It's fun to invite animals to your yard. But you can go to them too! Nature provides the food and shelter animals need. You can meet them on their turf!

Attracting
BIRDS & BUGS

*B*irdhouses, nesting materials, and birdbaths all help attract birds. But food is the most effective! Most birds have favorite foods, just like you.

TYPES *of* BIRD FOOD

SEEDS

Many birds eat a **variety** of different seeds.

SUET

Suet is hardened fat. It attracts birds that eat insects.

GRAINS

Ducks and geese like wheat, barley, and oats. They'll also eat shredded lettuce.

NECTAR

Nectar is basically sugar water. It attracts hummingbirds.

Sugar Is the Very Best Bug Bait!

What foods can you use to attract bugs? Any food will do! Bugs are attracted to sugar. And nearly all foods have some sugar. Fruits, vegetables, honey, juice, and meat contain sugar. The bottom line? You can use nearly any food to attract bugs!

Bug Benefits

There are more than one million insect species. Most of them are helpful to humans. Helpful insects include predators, pollinators, and recyclers.

Ladybugs are great for farms and gardens. They are predators. They eat bugs that hurt plants. Bees are pollinators. They spread pollen from plant to plant. This makes fruits, vegetables, and other plants grow. Flies are recyclers. They help waste and trash **decompose**. What would we do without them?

TAKING CARE

------- of Birds & Bugs -------

*S*eeing birds and insects up close is amazing. It's a privilege we should never **abuse**. When we attract wild animals, we owe it to them to be kind. If we are kind, they will survive. Perhaps they will even visit us again!

If birds come to your feeder, do not frighten them. Be quiet and respectful while you watch them. The same goes for bugs. If you catch a bug, enjoy your time with it. But hold it carefully and let it go soon.

ARE YOU READY?

☑ **Check the Weather.** Check the forecast before you begin any outdoor adventure!

☑ **Dress Appropriately.** Dress in layers! Be prepared for a **variety** of temperatures.

☑ Bring Water. It's important to drink enough water, especially if it's hot out.

☑ Get Permission. Some of the activities in this book require adult **supervision**. When in doubt, ask for help!

Now let's get out and enjoy the great outdoors!

Materials

Here are some of the things you'll need.

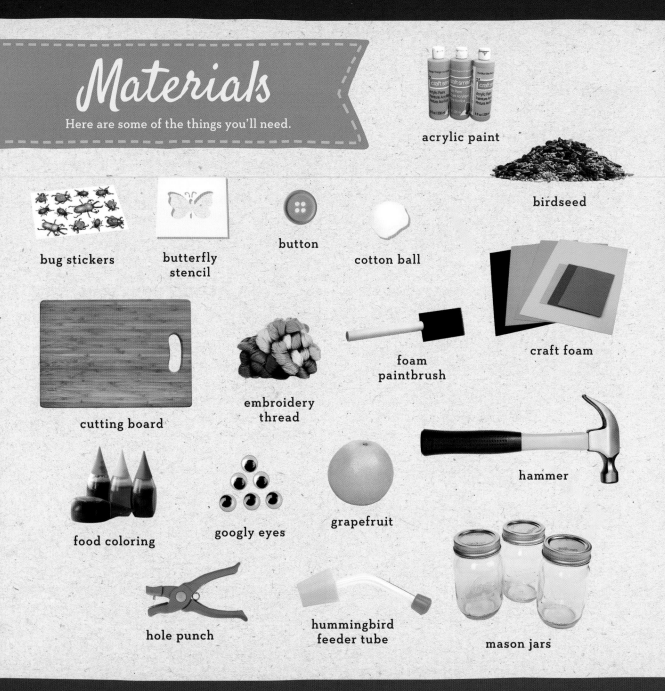

acrylic paint

birdseed

bug stickers

butterfly stencil

button

cotton ball

craft foam

cutting board

embroidery thread

foam paintbrush

food coloring

googly eyes

grapefruit

hammer

hole punch

hummingbird feeder tube

mason jars

measuring cups
& spoons

measuring tape

needle

notebook

panty hose

paper
towel tube

peanut butter

plastic bottle

puffy paint

ribbon

saucepan

sharp knife

suet holder

sugar

twine

wire

wooden craft
sticks

yarn

BEAUTIFUL bird's nest

Help your feathered friends make colorful nests!

Materials

yarn
ruler
scissors
suet holder

1 Cut the yarn into 2-inch (5 cm) pieces.

2 Open the suet holder. Put the yarn inside. Pack the holder completely full. Close the suet holder.

3 Pull gently at the scraps of yarn. Make them stick out of the holder on all sides.

4 Hang the suet holder outside in the sun.

TIP

March is the best time to hang up the holder. Birds make nests in early spring.

brilliant bird
FEEDER

Roll out the bird food!

Materials

paper towel tube
ruler
scissors
2 wooden craft sticks
hole punch
. place mat
peanut butter
dinner knife
birdseed
ribbon

1 Measure 2 inches (5 cm) from one end of the tube. Cut a 1/2-inch (1 cm) **horizontal** slit. Cut another slit directly across from the first one.

2 Repeat step 1 on the other end of the tube. Push a craft stick through each pair of slits.

3 Punch one hole 1/2 inch (1 cm) from each end of the tube.

4 Cover your work surface with a place mat. Spread peanut butter all over the tube. Do not cover the sticks. Cover the peanut butter with birdseed.

5 Cut a piece of ribbon 36 inches (91 cm) long. Push one end down through one hole in the tube. Then push it up through the other hole. Tie the ends together. Hang the bird feeder outside.

TIP

Use a toilet paper tube to make a mini feeder!

super citrus
FEEDER

Make a fun feeder that birds will love!

Materials

grapefruit
sharp knife
cutting board
spoon
string
ruler
scissors
large sewing needle
measuring cups and spoons
1 cup birdseed
2 tablespoons peanut butter
mixing bowl
mixing spoon

SHARP!

1 Cut the grapefruit in half. Scoop out the inside of the grapefruit. Cut four strings 15 inches (38 cm) long. Tie a knot at one end of each string.

2 Thread a string onto the sewing needle. Push the needle through the grapefruit near the edge. Go from the inside of the grapefruit to the outside. Pull until the knot hits the fruit. Remove the needle.

3 Repeat step 2 with the other three strings. Space them evenly around the grapefruit.

4 Put the birdseed and peanut butter in a bowl. Stir them together. Fill the grapefruit with the mixture.

5 Tie the ends of the strings together. Hang up your bird feeder.

TIP

Try this with other citrus fruits such as oranges or lemons!

FEED THE
butterflies

**Attract nature to
your backyard!**

Materials

large mason jar with metal lid
large nail
hammer
newspaper
tape
butterfly stencil
paint and paintbrush
twine
scissors
measuring tape
measuring cups and spoons
1 tablespoon sugar
saucepan
mixing spoon
red food coloring
large cotton ball

HOT!

SHARP!

1   Screw the lid onto the jar. Gently punch a hole in the center of the lid with a nail. Remove the lid.

2   Cover your work surface with newspaper. Turn the jar upside down. Tape a stencil to the glass. Paint over the stencil. Carefully remove the stencil. Let the paint dry. Paint more butterflies on the jar.

3   Cut five pieces of twine 36 inches (91 cm) long. Wrap one piece around the neck of the jar three times. Tie a knot. Cut off the extra twine.

(continued on next page)

TIP

June through September is the best time to attract butterflies.

4 Tie one end of each piece of twine to the twine around the jar. Space the twine pieces evenly around the jar.

5 Group the twine into pairs. Tie a knot in each pair. Make the knots 3 inches (8 cm) from the neck of the jar.

6 Separate the ends of the twine. Pair each piece of twine with one from the other knot. Tie the pairs together 3 inches (8 cm) from the previous knots.

7   Repeat step 6 to make another set of knots.

8   Gather the ends of the twine above the jar. Tie them together.

9   Put the sugar and 6 cups of water in a saucepan. Bring it to a boil over medium-high heat. Stir until the sugar is **dissolved**.

10 Fill the jar with the sugar mixture. Stir in red food coloring.

11 Pull the cotton ball halfway through the hole in the lid. Screw the lid on the jar tightly. Hang the jar upside down outside.

TIP

The feeder liquid spoils quickly. Be sure to change it and the cotton ball every few days.

hummingbird
FEEDER

Materials

acrylic paint
paper plate
pencil
small plastic bottle
red craft foam
scissors
hot glue gun & glue sticks
measuring tape
2 wires, 30 inches (76 cm) long
duct tape
measuring cups
½ cup sugar
saucepan
mixing spoon
hummingbird feeder tube

HOT!

1 Put a little paint on a paper plate. Dip the pencil's eraser in the paint. Use it to paint dots on the plastic bottle. Let the paint dry.

2 Cut small flowers out of the foam. Glue the flowers all around the bottle.

3 Lay the bottle on its side. Lay one piece of wire under the lip of the bottle. Lay the other wire on top of the bottle. Line it up with the first wire.

4 Twist the wires together on each side. Twist until about 4 inches (10 cm) of untwisted wire remains on each side.

5 Gather the ends of the wire under the bottom of the bottle. Twist them together. Tape the wires to the sides of the bottle.

6 Put the sugar and 1 cup of water in a saucepan. Bring it to a boil over medium-high heat. Stir until the sugar is **dissolved**. Pour the mixture into the bottle. Push the feeder tube into the bottle opening. Hang the feeder upside down.

backyard bug
JOURNAL

Materials

small notebook
button
pushpin
needle
embroidery thread
acrylic paint, several colors
paintbrush
black marker
tiny googly eyes
craft glue

SHARP!

1 Put the button on the top of the notebook. Poke the pushpin through the holes. Make holes in the notebook cover.

2 Thread the needle with embroidery thread. Tie a knot near the end. Push the needle up through one of the holes. Push it through a hole in the button. Pull until the knot hits the cover.

3 Push the needle down through a different hole in the button. Push it through the matching hole in the cover. Pull it tight. Repeat with the other holes to sew the button to the cover. Tie the ends of the thread together. Cut off the extra thread.

4 Paint your thumb. Make a **thumbprint** on the cover. Make more thumbprints with other colors of paint. Let the paint dry.

5 Use the marker to add legs to each thumbprint. Add antennas too. Make them look like bugs. Glue googly eyes onto the bugs.

build your own
BUG JAR

Materials

green paper
scissors
craft glue
mason jar
puffy paint
acrylic paint
paintbrush
bug stickers
panty hose
pencil
leaves

1   Cut green paper to look like grass. Glue it around the bottom of the jar.

2   Paint the word "Bugs" on the jar. Remove the center of the jar's lid. Paint the rim. Let the paint dry.

3   Decorate the jar with bug stickers. Put them on the sides of the jar.

4   Cut a rectangle out of the panty hose. Lay the center of the lid on the rectangle. Trace around it. Cut out the circle. Glue the circle inside the lid's rim. Let the glue dry.

5   Screw the lid on the jar. Put leaves and the bugs you catch inside the jar.

TIP   Only keep bugs in the jar a short time. Then release them outside.

How Great Is the GREAT OUTDOORS?

Did you enjoy making things for birds and bugs? Did any of the activities in this book inspire you to do more things in the great outdoors?

There is so much to love about being outside. These activities are just the beginning! Check out the other books in this series. You just might start spending more time outside than inside!

GLOSSARY

abuse – to use wrongly or too much.

appropriately – in a manner that is suitable, fitting, or proper for a specific occasion.

decompose – to break down or rot.

dissolve – to mix with a liquid so that it becomes part of the liquid.

horizontal – in the same direction as the ground, or side-to-side.

permission – when a person in charge says it's okay to do something.

supervision – the act of watching over or directing others.

thumbprint – the mark made by the ridges in the skin on a thumb.

variety – different types of one thing.

vitamin – a substance needed for good health, found naturally in plants and meats.

Websites

To learn more about Cool Great Outdoors, visit **booklinks.abdopublishing.com**. These links are routinely monitored and updated to provide the most current information available.

Index